A CELEBRATION
IN WORDS
AND PAINTINGS

SELECTED BY
HELEN EXLEY

≣EXLEY
MT. KISCO, NEW YORK • WATFORD, UK

The speed with which the world's children took to the Teddy Bear was nothing short of amazing, and soon the little creatures were making friends all round the globe - and of all ages, too.... In a remarkably short space of time it was quite clear that something more than just a toy had been created: the Teddy Bear became recognized as a symbol of love and affection that exerted a fascination for adults, too...Today, as the output worldwide shows no sign of decreasing, it is probably fair to say that the Teddy Bear's appeal has outlived and outlasted all other mascot animals.

PHILIPPA AND PETER WARING,
FROM *"TEDDY BEARS"*

●

No creature, round or scrawny, silly or sage, existing on the page or the nursery shelf, has captured the heart quite so well as the teddy bear. Toy makers and story tellers have given us collections of rabbits and cats, mice and ducks - but none has been loved so well or so long as Bear. I think it must be because, ever brave and courteous, loving and patient, he appeals to all the very best of human nature.

PATSY GRAY

●

... it is easy to overlook the fact that commercially Teddy has been the world's most successful toy.

CAROL ANN STANTON

●

A Bear is as alive as you need him to be.

PETER GRAY

•

Now when you come to consider [that teddy bears talk to you] you realize that this experience is, in fact, a feeling within you that is aroused by your sight of the teddy bear, though it speaks to you only in the sense of the significance it has for you, and this is largely connected with its form, which is that of a bear cub, soft and cuddly, so it appeals to your hunting and maternal, or paternal, instincts. The Teddy does not, of course, actually speak to you. It only seems to do so, because in your mind you imagine it does. By means of its subtle appeal the teddy bear excites your imagination....

PHILIPPA AND PETER WARING

•

A Teddy Bear does not depend upon mechanics or electronics to give him the semblance of life. He is loved - and therefore he lives.

PAM BROWN, b.1928

Teddy bears, with their plush, huggable bodies and amiable expressions, seem to possess an endearing quality of listening without judging. They bring out the best in us by fostering feelings of comfort, trust and love. Teddies, with their soothing faces, help the young and the old - and those somewhere in between - get through difficult times of sickness and need.

BO NILES,
FROM *"COUNTRY BEARS"*

THE PROTECTOR

Bears sleep by day. At night they stay awake to chase away bad dreams.

JESSE O'NEILL

•

I think about the times during my travels that I've awakened in the night in some strange hotel room, disoriented until I recognized one of my bears sitting nearby, like a sentry. It doesn't matter where I am; if there are teddies nearby, I know that I am safe.

TED MENTON,
FROM "THE TEDDY BEAR LOVER'S COMPANION"

•

Wake in the deepest dark of night and hear the driving rain.
Reach out a hand and take a paw and go to sleep again.

CHARLOTTE GRAY, b.1937

•

When all the world's against you - Ted is on your side.

JENNY DE VRIES

If you can trust no one else - you can always trust Bear.

PAM BROWN, b.1928

I love my bears, and when I am good to them they love me back. Actually, they love me even when I'm not good because that is the nature of Teddy Bears.

TED MENTON

...He's never cross or quick to carp
A friend in need is he to me.
When human tongues are mean and sharp
My Teddy gives me sympathy.

JEFFREY S. FORMAN,
TO COMMEMORATE THE TEDDY'S 75TH BIRTHDAY

A true bear never changes - stays constant through the years. A little worn, perhaps, a little touched by moth. Darned in places. Eccentric of eye and paw pad. But in his heart the same bear that he always was. Loyal. A keeper of secrets. A friend forever.

MARION C. GARRETTY, b.1917

●

Age simply doesn't enter into it! The older the friend, the more he is valued, particularly when he shows so visibly the characteristics that we all look for in friends. You have only to look at a genuine Teddy's face to see at once the loyalty, common sense, and, above all, dependability behind it.

PETER BULL

●

In a world where Best Friends come and go with unnerving rapidity, it is good for a child to come home to a friend who never varies in affection and goodwill.

PETER GRAY

●

THE HELPERS

Many unique teddy bears have been produced in recent times to help children with special needs. There are bears designed to help fretful babies sleep: The Kamar Toy Co.'s Dear Heart bear has a battery operated heart that beats like a human mother's. There is also a bear made to help the profoundly deaf, whose red eyes light up on hearing words. In Britain, Bill Bear was designed for chemical-sensitive children by Mary Holden, a fellow sufferer. Teddy bears have also proved a powerful support in distressing situations. In one French hospital, for example, prior to surgery, children are guided through an operation, using their teddy bears as patients, to help disband fear. In the United States, the Colorado police use the Celestial Seasonings Tea Co.'s Sleepy Time Bear to help young victims of accident and abuse.

PAULINE COCKRILL,
FROM *"THE ULTIMATE TEDDY BEAR BOOK"*

SAVE A BEAR...

For Bears of Character you need to search the auction sales. Poor souls - how have they come to be evicted from the ends of beds and cushioned comfort in the best armchair? What edict drove them forth? What awful change of heart and character? At least they did not end up in a refuse sack - the worst thing that can befall a bear. Like slaves sold down the river they shiver on the trestle tables. The dealers feel their ears to find the button that will declare them valuable - and toss them to one side. Legs in the air, all dignity lost, they wait. How can you leave him there, this disconsolate, battered bear? For the price of a cup of coffee, you can take him home, you can gain a life companion. Someone who will listen to your troubles with the understanding only granted to bears of great experience. A cup of coffee.

And see he's comfortable inside your shopping bag. He's had a most awful day.

JUDITH C. GRANT

COMFORTERS

Bears do not like to be lent.
Save to very small children in very
great distress.

HELEN THOMSON, b.1943

●

This phenomenon is, in fact, so intense, so
widespread, and so utterly taken for granted by
adults, many of whom adhere to it themselves,
that it demands some investigation both
psychologically and mythologically for the bear,
in the form of the teddy-bear has, oddly it
seems, become our society's comforter. That
almost all-pervading cuddly creature, which, for
many children is more important than any doll,
and which remains with so many adults as
something at once intrinsic and marginal to
their most intimate life, acts in loco parentis as
an archetypal mother/father understander-of-all,
as indeed an original comforter, or Paraclete.

EITHNE KAISER

●

A bear has no great depth of mind
- but yet is patient, quiet and kind.
One does not need a massive brain
to comfort friends in fear or pain.

CHARLOTTE GRAY

•

Bears need people. People need bears.

PAM BROWN, b.1928

BATTERED BY LOVE

...does maturity mean abandoning our beloved teddy bears, and truest childhood friends, or does it mean being strong enough to proudly proclaim our devotion to them? If I had to

choose, there would be no contest - the kind of maturity that has no room for whimsy is meaningless and offers no reward. Give me the warmth of a tattered teddy any day.

TED MENTON,
FROM *"THE TEDDY BEAR LOVER'S COMPANION"*

●

The more a bear has been loved, the more children whose companion he has been, the more venerable and prized he is. He becomes like an elderly relative of the household rather than being an object of childhood memories. He is a constant link in a chain of love, his position and status similar to that of a pagan household god, protecting successive generations.

GENEVIÈVE AND GÉRARD PICOT,
FROM *"TEDDY BEARS"*

●

Newer, *novice* bears, express the love of a child, while *experienced* bears convey the warmth and tenderness only age can bring.

TED MENTON,
FROM *"THE TEDDY BEAR LOVER'S CATALOGUE"*

●

LOST AND ABANDONED

One never *quite* gets over a lost bear.

JANE SWAN

•

A lost bear needs to go to the police
station.
They are very kind there to bears
in distress.

ROSANNE AMBROSE-BROWN

•

Toys in car boot sales are just that. Save for
Bears who are Displaced Persons.

J. R. COULSEN

•

I hope one day we meet up with all the lost
Teddy Bears again - and the little lost cats.
And the grandads and grandmas.
What a hugging that will be!

HELEN THOMSON, b.1943

•

POPULATION EXPLOSION!

Since the creation of the first Teddy Bear in the early years of this century...his popularity has grown to such an extent that it is estimated that the annual world figure for the sale of Teddy Bears is in excess of £30 million, and may well be getting nearer £50 million by the minute. (It's $40 million dollars every year in America alone at the moment!) That represents an almost incalculable number of large and small, thin and fat, furry and cuddly, dressed and undressed, brown, black, white...multi-featured Teddy Bears pouring from almost every nation on the face of the earth.

The number of Teddies of all ages still in existence must indeed be legion. For Teddy

Bears do not die, only love and affection causes them to wear away. People just don't part with them like other toys - nor do they very often sell them, which accounts for the rarity and collectability of the older types.

If we may illustrate the point further, in 1972 it was reported that in the United Kingdom alone 63.8% of all households contained one or more Teddy Bears....

PHILIPPA AND PETER WARING

●

What a miracle life is, and how whimsical that in all their wonder and their pain, their confusion and their joy, human beings had the idea to create teddy bears to keep them company and help them make it through the hard times.

TED MENTON

This infiltration by the Teddy Bear into our lives has been very subtle, achieved almost without most of us being aware of the fact. And it is only when you sit down and take stock of how widely he features in everyday life that some idea of the extent of his influence emerges.

There is a whole library of books about fictional Teddies, of course, and he's been featuring in films, television, and on radio not to mention in newspapers, magazines, comics and in advertizing pretty consistently over the past three quarters of a century. He's had songs written about him, poetry composed in his honour and his likeness has appealed to numerous artists and cartoonists. For years he's been one of the most popular characters on birthday and post cards. Teddies have raised fortunes for charities, been promotional free gifts, appeared as the showpieces of exhibitions, and delighted thousands of all ages at rallies, picnics and all manner of fund raising activities. ... He has been a lucky mascot at more types of sporting events than any other stuffed toy.

PHILIPPA AND PETER WARING

Do you love your Teddy? Do you carry him with you, talk to him secretly, cuddle him when you're feeling down? Are you forty-five? Be not ashamed. The day of the arctophile liberation is close at hand.... Millions of grown-ups treasure their battered, eyeless, one-eared, furry little friends. The closet doors are about to spring open and arctophiles will pour forth.

VICKIE MACKENZIE

•

Sometimes when I'm describing some of Theodore's foibles or quirks I see a look of terror come into the eyes of the listener. For it is usually incomprehensible to the person who has never possessed or even wanted a Teddy Bear that an *adult* can be so passionately attached to what is apparently only a stuffed toy. But then I feel the same sort of thing when people start going on about their cars, yachts, houses, or bank balances, all of which seem to me far more inanimate than Teddy.

PETER BULL

•

Children don't understand why a relationship with a Teddy is apt to be so much more rewarding than with an animal, but it is easy for *us* to see why. Teddies don't mind being taken for a walk, beaten about, dressed in ridiculous hats (at least they don't complain *aloud!*), or even being read to. There are no jealousies or other emotional upheavals to contend with - no pressure, no guilt. And not only do Teddies seem to be more *satisfactory* to get involved with than real animals, but there are also cases of their even superseding humans entirely because of their qualities.

PETER BULL

●

Cats versus Bears?
The differences are:
Bears aren't picky over their dinners.
Bears don't fuss when they fall out of bed.
Bears don't sulk. (Much.)
Bears aren't always on the wrong side of the door.
Bears don't run up vets' bills
- all you need is a needle and thread.

PAM BROWN, b.1928

A HAPPY
XMAS TO YOU

TEDDIES BY THE HUNDRED

"Why do people collect teddy bears?" People who keep company with bears are often not really *collectors* but rather *lovers*.... True, there are many people who have vast dens of bears numbering in the hundreds and even thousands, but even these aficionados differ from the usual *collector*. Often the bears in these collections have no real monetary value as collectibles. Their charm is their ability to amuse and to create a sense of loving. It is equally true that there are many bears that have come to be

valuable in terms of dollars, but whose intrinsic value still seems to be emotional.

TED MENTON

●

Collector Claudette Latchford ... nicknamed Teddy since she was at school, has been collecting bears for 26 years. She now has over 700, but her favourite is still her first childhood friend. "Teddy was always there when I needed him," she recalls. "Even today, when I'm fed up or upset, I'll go to Teddy."

Claudette's collection ranges from a gold-plated bear standing a quarter of an inch high, to Becket, a Canterbury Bear who weighs over four stone and is nearly six feet tall. Each is given a name and carefully catalogued. As well as over 450 soft bears, Claudette has them in gold, silver, bread, chocolate and marzipan. The oldest are German and Swiss carved bears dating from the Victorian period, but even the lamp in the sitting room and the telephone on Claudette's desk are bear-shaped....

JILLIAN POWELL

●

POOR BEAR!

There is probably nothing that a bear so dislikes as A Good Wash.

MARION C. GARRETTY, b.1917

•

Bears being sent through the mail should never be squashed up to make them fit. It gives them indigestion.

PAM BROWN, b.1928

•

Contrary to belief, bears do not appreciate being fed with honey or jam sandwiches. They know it heralds soap and water and spending the morning hanging from the clothes-line by one ear.

JESSE O'NEILL

•

A bear's chief nightmare is being left behind.

ALEX LEVY

•

FURRY BEAR

If I were a bear,
   And a big bear too,
I shouldn't much care
   If it froze or snew;
I shouldn't much mind
   If it snowed or friz -
I'd be all fur-lined
   With a coat like his!
For I'd have fur boots and a brown fur wrap,
And brown fur knickers and a big fur cap.
I'd have a fur muffle-ruff to cover my jaws,
And brown fur mittens on my big brown paws.
With a big brown furry-down up to my head,
I'd sleep all the winter in a big fur bed.

A. A. MILNE (1882-1956)

Bear, Bear, don't go away
To come again some other day
I will love you if you stay
I will love you any way.

VICTORIAN GREETING CARD

...A bear, however hard he tries,
Grows tubby without exercise.
Our Teddy Bear is short and fat,
Which is not to be wondered at.
But do you think it worries him
To know that he is far from slim?
No, must the other way about -
He's proud of being short and stout.

A. A. MILNE (1882-1956)

A BIG JOB FOR LITTLE BEARS

Giving bears to hospital patients has long been a tradition among teddy bear lovers. Many groups do this good work, but I guess the most famous is *Good Bears of the World,* which has bear dens worldwide. Today, inspired by the good deeds of others, I bring bears to hospitals to work with terminally ill children. The children come from across the country for treatment; their parents and friends are often thousands of miles away. The bears and I do our best to make the kids a little happier. I tell stories, but the bears do the real work - they watch over the children at difficult times. In these kids' lives lurks a very real boogeyman, and the children all know that his name is Death. It's a big job for little bears, but they manage because they are filled with love - the love they're endowed with by children.

TED MENTON,
FROM *"THE TEDDY BEAR LOVER'S COMPANION"*

GREAT SURVIVORS

The Bluebird was travelling at some 365 miles
per hour when the vehicle encountered a patch
of wet salt. The car went out of control and was
airborne for more than a thousand feet during
which time it was performing the most
extraordinary aerobatic manoeuvres and finally
ended up a total wreck some three quarters of a
mile from where it left the course. I survived
with a fractured skull and lying in hospital
some four hours later, realized with horror that
Mr. Woppit was still in the cockpit. An urgent
radio message was despatched and Mr. Woppit
accorded a police escort from the flats to the
hospital. He was examined on arrival but was
found to have survived with nothing worse than
a nose out of joint!

**DONALD CAMPBELL,
WORLD WATER-SPEED CHAMPION**

Teddies go everywhere and do everything. There is not a corner of the globe that they have not penetrated, if not with children then with adults. Their appeal is universal and to all ages. They have gone into battle on guns, tanks and in haversacks; saved lives by intercepting bullets; flown all over the world in aeroplanes; been "drowned" in floods, burned in concentration camps and worshipped as Totems; are used extensively in advertising campaigns; collected by film stars, ballerinas and actresses; used as mascots and talismans; had endless books, songs and verses written about them; are taken to hospital, are indeed part of our everyday life - and all within the space of sixty years!

MARGARET HUTCHINGS,
FROM *"THE BOOK OF THE TEDDY BEAR"*

●

There are no cases of disloyal, treacherous, or cowardly Teddy Bears. They seem destined to survive everything, and emerge as a triumphant symbol of something or other.

PETER BULL

●

IT'S FOR LIFE!

Every child has his Pooh, but one would think it odd if every man still kept his Pooh to remind him of his childhood. But my Pooh is different, you say. He is *the* Pooh. No, this only makes him different to you, not different to me. My toys were and are to me no more than yours were and are to you.

CHRISTOPHER MILNE,
FROM *"THE ENCHANTED PLACES"*

•

On my only daughter's second birthday, she was given a large doll and a big brown teddy-bear. Thirty years later they are still in her old room.

Her two little girls often play with them and on their last visit the eldest one wanted to take the teddy-bear home. "No," said my daughter. "She can't do that - it's mine!"

MRS. SMITH,
FROM A LETTER IN *"THE SUNDAY PEOPLE"*, 1979

•

WHO, EXACTLY, LIKES TEDDIES?

There's no such thing as an average teddy bear fancier, or arctophile. I'm constantly surprised by the stories I hear and the people I meet. There are sober-suited businessmen who take their bears to hotels or guesthouses to be looked after while they're away, and it has even been known for people to take their bears on holiday, give them passports and pay for seats on the plane for them! Some owners take their bears to restaurants, but then of course there is Clarence, the Marquess of Bath's bear, who sits at the head of the table at Longleat, and the bear at Blenheim Palace who regularly makes up the number for dinner parties!

SUE CLEEVE, EDITOR OF *"TEDDY BEAR TIMES"*

●

There probably isn't one among us who can't remember the comforting effect of cuddling up to a teddy bear at night.

RACHEL NEWMAN,
FROM *"COUNTRY BEARS"*

During the fifteen years or so in which I have been connected with the dear creatures I have met many fascinating, warm and totally sane people. I can't remember meeting anyone interested in the phenomenon of the Teddy who was bitter, unpleasant or downright beastly.

PETER BULL,
FROM *"A HUG OF TEDDY BEARS"*

●

...wasn't a certain younger son of a certain queen accused of sleeping with a teddy bear at the foot of his bed, even at the age of twenty-two?

GENEVIÈVE AND GÉRARD PICOT,
FROM *"TEDDY BEARS"*

●

A NEW LIFE

They went up into the attic only a little while
ago. It seemed urgent. They'd weathered
porridge and linctus, expeditions entailing mud
and sand, nights beneath the stars, days in a
thin, cold drizzle of rain. Measles. Flu. And
fights. A kitten. A large, strange dog. Under-
bed fluff. Moths. Sticky kisses. Peggings to the
clothes-line. They'd been retired with dignity.
Moth-balled, admittedly - which no true bear
should have to suffer - but put away with room
to breathe. They seem resigned. And now a
little flustered. For someone's clicked on the
light. Someone's searched through the boxes.
"Here they are. Father Bear and Fred the Red
Ted and Blue and Scruff and Nelson. I'll drop
them down. Catch." A heart-stopping flight
through empty air - but safely caught. And
smiles and half-familiar voices.

A box. A car. A stair. A nursery.
And life begins again.

B. R. MEADOWS, b.1966

A LOVE THAT LASTS

I stretch, swing my backpack of bears over my shoulder and head for the [hospital] exit. In the hallway, an old gentleman shuffles along with a walker. As I pass beside him, he calls to me.

"You the teddy-man?" he asks in a voice that seems to shake his feeble frame. "The fellow with the bears?"

"Yes, I am."

"That's good work. Really helps. Really does."
His eyes brighten and his voice gets stronger. "I
had a teddy but I gave him to my grandson.
That bear helped me grow up, kept me company,
made me laugh, and he really loved me. I gave
him to my grandson so he could go on doing his
job. Yes siree, givin' love, that's a bear's work."

He reaches out and takes my arm. "You
wouldn't happen to have a little bear in there
that might want to live in an old man's bathrobe
pocket, I don't suppose?"

TED MENTON,
FROM *"THE TEDDY BEAR LOVER'S COMPANION"*

●

One of the saddest duties I have to perform is
to reassure elderly people who are disturbed
about what will become of their loyal beloved
friends of many years' standing, should
anything happen to the so-called owner. Some
even go to the length of leaving instructions in
their will that they should be buried or
cremated together.

PETER BULL,
FROM *"A HUG OF TEDDY BEARS"*

●

EVERYONE LOVES BEARS

It has been argued in some quarters that the reason for the Teddy Bear's success was that it came onto the market at a time when there was a great need for a toy for boys, dolls being considered unsuitable for them. Just as dolls appealed to the feminine and maternal instincts in girls, so the toy bears appealed to the masculine, hunting and parental instincts in boys. What really happened, of course, was that both sexes found the little creatures absolutely irresistible!

PHILIPPA AND PETER WARING

Adults have a definite and equal need for the dear creatures. There is a vast underground Teddy bear movement. We arctophiles are a touchy lot, and insults or ridicule by ignorant persons puts our hackles up. One is Teddy bear conscious in the same way other people are car, garden, clothes, food or cat conscious.

PETER BULL

A HAPPY ENDING

Once upon a time, there was a bear who had been loved almost to extinction. He had lost his black nose very early on, and someone had replaced it with a little circle of red felt. His name was Spot. His friend's mother was a Very Sensible Woman and when his friend got to be six she told him the time for bears was over. Which sounds plausible, but is, nevertheless, not true. His friend sat and looked at Spot and thought about graves in the garden and garage sales and bonfires. And - when his sensible mother was not around - he cried a little. But then his aunt came to tea and he took her to one side when his mother was out in the kitchen, and he asked if she knew of any little boy who wanted a bear. And would take great care of it, and love it. And she said she did. The very next day she had a word with a little boy with a loving heart, whose mother was, alas, *far* from sensible. And that is how Spot came to live with us. He's been here for twenty-five years now - and I'm glad to say is extremely fit and well. If a little faded in complexion. And waiting to go to live with a new baby. Who will, it is to be hoped, be as non-sensible about bears as her papa.

PAM BROWN, b.1928

A bear teaches us that if the heart is true, it doesn't much matter if an ear drops off.

HELEN EXLEY, b.1943

●

There is something impressive about bears whose exteriors are really nothing but a tissue of scars, some stitched up clumsily, their seams bulging and distended, others showing the signs of expert attention, stitched together in matching thread almost invisible to the eye.

GENEVIÈVE AND GÉRARD PICOT,
FROM *"TEDDY BEARS"*

●

Bears are not like human beings. They look upon newness as an embarrassment, and youth as an apprenticeship, and baldness as a most honorable estate. A bear glories in a restitched nose, a patched paw, an eye that has been replaced by a button. These things prove that it is loved. That it is a Real Bear.

PAM BROWN, b.1928

●

A TOUCH OF SANITY

Edward Bear...permeates the whole structure of society. This is because he is a truly international figure who is nonreligious and yet universally recognized as a symbol of love. He represents friendship, and so is a powerful instrument of good will, a wonderful ambassador of peace, functioning as a leavening influence amid the trials and tribulations of life in the modern world.

COLONEL BOB HENDERSON

●

In a world gone bad, a bear - even a bear standing on its head - is a comforting, uncomplicated, dependable hunk of sanity.

PAM BROWN, b.1928

●

...the bear has commanded a special place in folklore, myth, fairy-tale and legend...today, in the form of the Teddy Bear, it is grasped in psychic compensation and clung to for security...history, religion, philosophy and psychology are all involved in any proper explanation of the mystique of the Teddy Bear.

COLONEL BOB HENDERSON

•

World Government Needs Bears.

HELEN EXLEY, b.1943

•

What is the Teddy's special appeal that has made him survive as number one toy through wars and recessions? Questioned recently, some Teddy bear owners suggested that bears appealed because they "looked" at you, while others thought that Teddies "listened".

MARY HILLIER

•

What is it about the Teddy Bear which gives it this fantastic appeal? This is without doubt one of the most interesting psychological questions about the history of toys.

LADY ANTONIA FRASER,
FROM *A HISTORY OF TOYS*

•

I ... even wish I could shed some light on the reason why we love our bears and find their companionship so delightful. But all that is rather like explaining what the Grand Canyon looks like as the first rays of dawn illuminate its walls...you have to be there.

TED MENTON,
FROM *THE TEDDY BEAR LOVER'S CATALOGUE*

•